# THE BEANO PRANKIPEDIA

## THE GREATEST PRANKS, HOAXES AND JAPES...IN HISTORY!

PUFFIN

ENACE SCENE-DO NOT CROSS

PUFFIN BOOKS
Published by the Penguin Group: London, New York, Australia,
Canada, India, Ireland, New Zealand and South Africa
Penguin Books Ltd, Registered Offices: 80 Strand, London
WC2R 0RL, England

puffinbooks.com

First published 2014
001

Written by Dean Wilkinson
Illustrations by Nigel Parkinson
Image Credits:
Page 11 - © Landmarkmedia
Page 15 – © NASA Images
Page 31 – © Bocman1973 / Shutterstock.com
Page 48 – © Andy Lidstone

Made and printed in China
ISBN: 978–0–141–35598–6

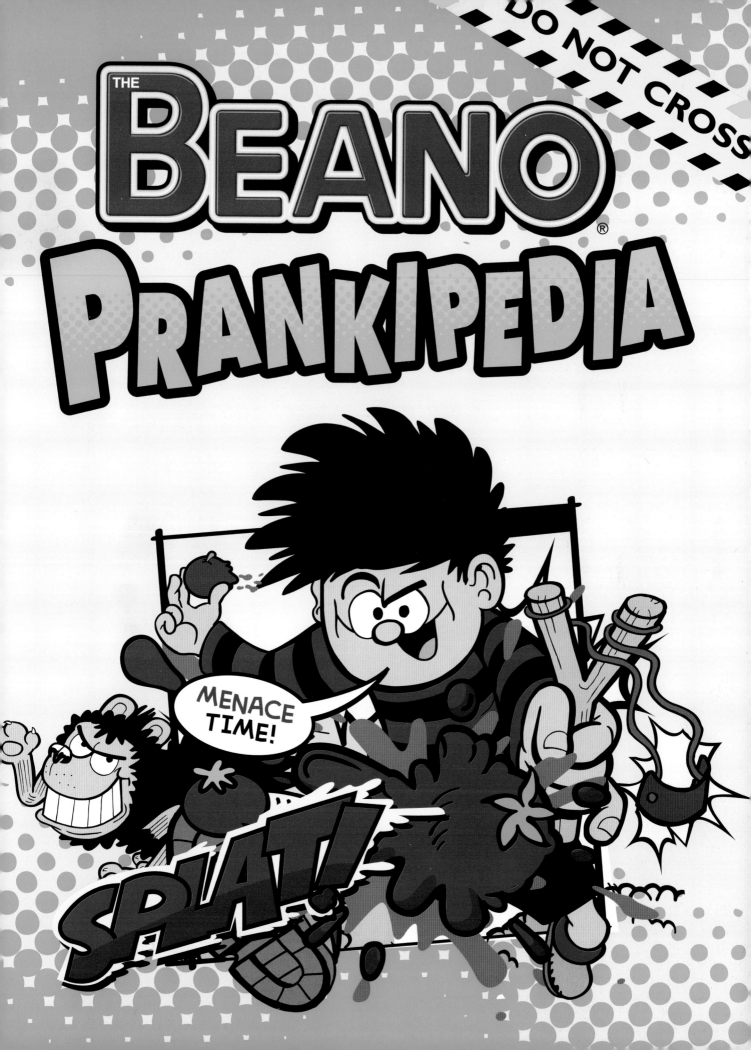

# CONTENTS

| | |
|---|---|
| **Welcome to Your PranKipedia!** | 6 |
| **How This Book Works** | 7 |
| **COSMIC CONS** | 8 |
| The First Great Moon Hoax | 10 |
| Moore or Less Gravity? | 11 |
| Alien Autopsy | 12 |
| Come a Cropper | 13 |
| The Martians Have Landed! | 14 |
| The Second Great Moon Hoax | 15 |
| **PRANKY PEOPLE** | 16 |
| Marathon Man Come Home | 18 |
| Honey, the Kid Blew Away! | 19 |
| An Aussie Iceberg? Strewth! | 20 |

| | |
|---|---|
| Operation Mincemeat | 21 |
| World's Greatest Artist? | 22 |
| Volcano High Jinks | 23 |
| The Piltown Let Down | 24 |
| Disney on Ice? | 25 |
| Faking His Own Death... By Dying | 26 |
| Gregg Jevin Went to Heaven | 27 |
| **FOODIE FAKES** | 28 |
| The Spaghetti Harvest | 30 |
| Cola Claus? | 31 |
| Whistling Carrots | 32 |
| Crisps Crum's? | 33 |
| **TECHNO TRICKERY** | 34 |

Big Ben Goes Digital 36

Internet Spring Clean 37

Tights TV 38

18th Century Chess Robot 39

Jelly Belly Fat Feet 40

Booby Trap 41

FABLES AND FANTASIES 42

Fairy Nuff! 44

Beware, the Loch Ness Hoaxster! 45

The Amityville Horror 46

The Cardiff Giant 47

Paul the Beatle is as Dead
as a Dodo 48

Fairy, Fairy Funny 49

Bigfoot, Big Fibs? 50

Ghost Takes Over TV! 51

BEASTLY BLUFFS 52

Incredible Flying Penguins 54

Fiji Fish Fingy 55

An Octopus to Look Up To! 56

Gef the Talking Mongoose 57

The Dogs Are All White 58

Zoo Must be Joking! 59

Finding the Fakes 60

Finding the Fakes (continued) 62

# WELCOME . . . TO YOUR

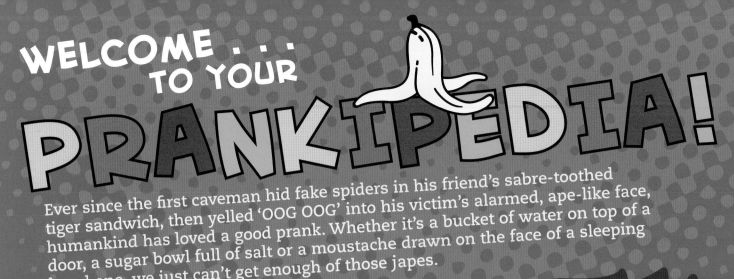

# PRANKIPEDIA!

Ever since the first caveman hid fake spiders in his friend's sabre-toothed tiger sandwich, then yelled 'OOG OOG' into his victim's alarmed, ape-like face, humankind has loved a good prank. Whether it's a bucket of water on top of a door, a sugar bowl full of salt or a moustache drawn on the face of a sleeping loved one, we just can't get enough of those japes.

Throughout history, all over the world, pranks have been an ever-present. There is no nation that doesn't enjoy seeing clingfilm stretched over a toilet. No culture that doesn't guffaw at a whoopee cushion left on grandma's favourite chair. No menace or minx who doesn't love a stinky stink bomb.

This book is all about those pranks that went above and beyond the call of duty. The big-time, heavy duty japes that made the news and spread like fake bogeys on a door handle. The April Fool's Day gags, the hoaxes, the scams, the urban legends: they're all here, in one big beautiful package.

So please settle down, give your best friend's unopened can of pop an almighty shake, and enjoy.

# HOW THIS BOOK WORKS

As well as filling you in on *The Beano* team's all-time favourite pranks, you'll probably notice that each page of your Prankipedia also has a few ace extras . . .

Minnie's Verdict

Dennis's Verdict

This is where Dennis and Minnie give their views on each prank. Was it a goody? Was it a baddy? Or was it just really weird? Menaces and minxes never hold back!

## SPLATISTICS

| SILLINESS | |
| --- | --- |
| IMPACT | |
| DARING | |
| OVERALL | |

How silly was the prank? How big an impact did it make? How daring was it? What's its overall score? The Splatistics give it to you straight, in handy splat-based form!

# COSMIC CONS

Space! Do you know it has three ears? The left ear, the right ear, and the final front ear. Har har. With all that empty, infinite blackness, there's plenty of room up there for a good prank or three. Here are some of the best ones . . .

BOING!

BOING!

SQUELCH!

# THE FIRST GREAT MOON HOAX

**Date: 1835**
**Place: USA**

Herds of space-buffalo. A round monster that rolls around beaches. Beavers that walk on two legs. A blue goat. Man-Bats! It can only mean one thing . . . life has been found on the Moon! When the New York Sun broke this story, it soon became the news of the world!

The paper reported that, thanks to his **super-powerful telescope**, astronomer Sir John Herschel had observed the creatures living on the lunar surface. The marvellous beasts were said to spend their time **munching on fruit**, bathing in lunar waters and generally having a right old laugh.

The only problem with this astounding story was . . . it was a **load of cobblers!** The paper made the whole thing up and hijacked Herschel's name to give the hoax credibility. Today, this amazing tale is regarded as one of the very first science fiction stories, and inspired many writers and artists to think seriously about the possibility of **alien life** for the first time.

## SPLATISTICS

SILLINESS
IMPACT
DARING
OVERALL

**Dennis's Verdict**

I've always thought Walter and his posse were from outer space. The Planet Bum-Face is my bet. He'd definitely have fitted in with those Man-Bat things too. What's the point of being an alien if you're just going to lie around eating fruit and bathing all day? If aliens do ever come to Earth, they'd better be huge bug-eyed menacing monsters with laser guns. That'd be SO cool!

# MOORE OR LESS GRAVITY?

**Date: 1976**
**Place: England**

## SPLATISTICS

| SILLINESS | |
| --- | --- |
| IMPACT | |
| DARING | |
| OVERALL | |

WORM JUICE

Sir Patrick Moore was a highly respected English astronomer who wrote over seventy books on the subject and presented the world's longest running telly show, *The Sky at Night*. Moore could come across as very official and serious (a bit like a grumpy teacher), but behind it all he had a wicked sense of humour.

On 1st April 1976, he made an **amazing announcement** during a radio interview. He said that, at 9.47 that morning, if you jumped in the air, you would be able to **float** because of a rare planetary alignment reducing the Earth's atmosphere. Moore explained that the lining up of Pluto, Jupiter and Earth would reduce our gravity for a moment so it was a **good time to have a float about**. At 9.47am exactly, he shouted, **'JUMP NOW!'**

The BBC was **inundated with callers** complaining that nothing had happened. But much **weirder** is the fact that many people also rang in to say how amazing it was! Even though there was no truth in it at all, they still said it had happened to them. A Dutch woman reckoned she and her husband had had **a jolly old float around their house**. One bloke even said he rose up so fast he **cracked his noggin on the ceiling**, and demanded compensation!

People still regard Moore's gravity gag as one of the best pranks ever. **Nice one, Sir Patrick** – you were one of a kind!

**Minnie's Verdict**

An interesting prank and I wondered if I could apply the physics of such a jovial theorem to minxing. I set up a laboratory and began working out the dynamics of the Moore-Gravity jape, equating it with the prime directive of minxing. After several minutes of mathematical tinkering I decided I didn't really understand what any of those words actually meant, so just waited for Fatty Fudge to come along and launched a water balloon at him. Genius!

# ALIEN AUTOPSY

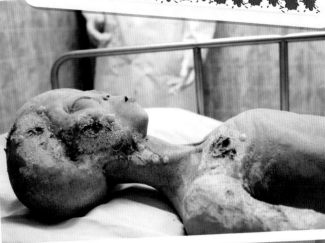

In 1947, an alien ship crashed in Roswell, New Mexico, and the bodies of the E.T.s were hidden away by the government. That's what conspiracy theorists believe, at least.

Years later, in 1995, grainy footage surfaced of a dead alien being chopped up by American surgeons. It was one of the **most gruesome bits of film** ever seen.

English record producer Ray Santilli claimed he'd bought the footage from a retired US Army photographer for a **massive wad of cash**. He wanted to prove to the world that we are **not alone** in the universe. But, in 2006, Ray admitted it was fake. The 'alien' was a **rubber model filled with chicken bits** and animal bones.

Weirdly though, Ray insisted that he bought **genuine alien autopsy footage**, but the film was in such poor condition that it became unwatchable – so he reconstructed it. Even now he claims a few frames in the fake are from the original. **The truth is out there!** Possibly.

DUTY FREE

**Winnie's Verdict**

Imagine if there really were aliens and they saw this film? They'd do their nut! They'd think the poor alien just popped down to Earth for a mini break and to pick up some duty free, only to end up deader than a sausage sandwich and being chopped up in a hospital. This Ray bloke has probably ruined the chances of any alien tourists ever visiting Earth now. I could have made a fortune selling cheap tat to gullible space tourists. I'll have to get a real job now.

**Date: 1970s**
**Place: England/Global**

# COME A CROPPER

BOING!
SQUELCH!

## SPLATISTICS

| SILLINESS | |
| --- | --- |
| IMPACT | |
| DARING | |
| OVERALL | |

Crop circles first started appearing in the 1970s, often in English fields near ancient stone monuments like Stonehenge. Before long, they were appearing in fields all over the world. Crops appeared flattened into mathematically perfect, alien-looking shapes and designs. As the phenomenon grew, the designs became more and more fancy.

**Dennis's Verdict**

I love crop circles! I even thought I spotted one recently. It was on my dad's head. It was a false alarm, though. It turns out it was just the start of a bald patch.

**What did it all mean?** Were spaceships landing in the dead of night and leaving weird tracks behind? Were aliens leaving messages for us in some intergalactic language that nobody could figure out? Actually, it was neither of those. In 1991, two pranksters admitted to making loads of the English ones. They 'fessed up to using **ropes and planks** to get perfect circles.

Since then, more and more people have come forward to claim responsibility for crop circles. Several people have even been prosecuted for vandalism! You see, the pranksters were actually committing a crime by destroying farmers' crops and putting their businesses in danger. **Not so clever now, is it?**

One theory commonly held nowadays is that the idea for creating crop circles came from naturally occurring patterns in grass and fields, sometimes called **fairy rings**. But that doesn't mean it's actually fairies that are behind them, before you ask!

13

# THE MARTIANS HAVE LANDED!

Date: 1938
Place: USA

On the night before Halloween (mischief night) in 1938, an episode of the weekly *Mercury Theatre on the Air* radio show broadcast an adaptation of the scary H.G. Wells novel *The War of the Worlds*. Parts of the Martian invasion story were presented like news bulletins to add to the tension. And it worked – a bit too well!

## SPLATISTICS

SILLINESS

IMPACT

DARING

OVERALL

You see, many listeners confused the drama for a news story announcing a **real-life Martian invasion**. And it terrified the breakfast out of them!

There was widespread panic, and the police were inundated with **frantic calls**. Was the end of the world nigh? It was even worse for the unfortunate residents of a Washington town named Concrete. By an amazing coincidence, Concrete's power failed at the time of the broadcast, plunging the locals into **darkness**.

Orson Welles, a **famous American actor**, was playing the part of the newsreader. While the play was going out live, reports started to come in about the **very real panic**. So the radio bosses made Orson stop the show and explain it had all been a big misunderstanding and wasn't real. Although this wasn't actually a deliberate prank, it's still regarded as **one of the best tricks ever played on the public**.

**Dennis's Verdict**

I can totally understand the panic those people felt, because something similar happened to me. Mum once told me it was bath night on a Saturday, thinking it was Sunday. I nearly fainted! So compared to what I went through, this is peanuts.

# THE SECOND GREAT MOON HOAX

## SPLATISTICS

| SILLINESS | |
| --- | --- |
| IMPACT | |
| DARING | |
| OVERALL | |

Even if you weren't around in 1969, the chances are you'll still know those famous words spoken by Neil Armstrong as he set foot on the Moon's surface. They are unforgettable. 'One small step for man . . . something something blah blah blah.'

NASA had actually put a man on the Moon! **Awesome!** Except . . . it was all a **big, fat, stinky lie!** Well, that's what a lot of people think, at least. They say the footage was created in a film studio here on Earth!

In some scenes, the astronauts appear to be on cables, enabling them to pretend they're **bouncing along in low gravity**. There's even a reflection that looks like a light from a film studio!

Of course, the whole thing begs one big blooming question: **why?** Well, at the time, the Americans were in a **space race** with the Russians. Russia had already **fired a man into space**, so America was keen to prove it was just as big and clever. Putting a man on the Moon would be like blowing a **big sloppy raspberry** at Russia. **Thrrrp!**

If the 1969 Moon landing was fake, then it has to be **THE greatest prank in the history of everything**. The jury is still out on this one.

Apollo 11¾

L. PRETEND

### Minnie's Verdict

I know for a fact that this Moon landing business is definitely a fake. I've seen the film footage of the rocket being launched. It was daytime! Hello! The Moon only comes out at night! Massive flaw in the plan there NASA, you big idiots! Come on guys, it's not rocket science!

# PRANKY PEOPLE

# MARATHON MAN COME HOME

Date: 1981
Place: England

## SPLATISTICS

| | |
|---|---|
| SILLINESS | |
| IMPACT | |
| DARING | |
| OVERALL | |

You have to be either very fit or very silly to run a marathon. Some people who do it are both, like the ones who run while dressed as a giant dog.

**BEANOTOWN MARATHON**
SPONSORED BY WINDY BEANS

0 0 0 1

In 1981, the *Daily Mail* announced that a Japanese man, Kimo Nakajimi, had entered the London Marathon and **slightly misunderstood the rules**. Instead of running the gruelling twenty-six miles, he thought he had to run for twenty-six days! So, while all the other competitors had finished, given up, or been rushed to hospital to have their fancy dress costumes surgically removed, Kimo kept going. He just **ran and ran and ran**. He was supposedly spotted all over England, **sweating and puffing his way around the countryside**. People tried to flag him down but he just waved back, nodding his thanks for their support. It's a brilliant story . . . but, sadly, it's also completely made up. It was another newspaper prank.

Speaking of marathons, did you know that several people have been banned from them for cheating? It's true! In 2012, a Sunderland man was barred from all future Great North Runs for allegedly **hopping on a bus**. And, in 1980, Boston Marathon winner Rosie Ruiz had her winner's medal **snatched back** when it was discovered she had taken a subway train! What a **big fibber**!

**Dennis's Verdict**

I've always thought marathons were a complete waste of time, but I do like to do my bit for charity. I was once sponsored to go up and down stairs a thousand times! Sounds exhausting, right? Well, it wasn't that tiring. Those escalators can be quite relaxing.

# HONEY, THE KID BLEW AWAY!

Date: 2009
Place: USA

## SPLATISTICS

| | |
|---|---|
| SILLINESS | |
| IMPACT | |
| DARING | |
| OVERALL | |

This one all started when an experimental weather balloon flew out of control. It had been built by Richard and Mayumi Heene, who were amateur weather watchers. The horrifying thing was, they said their six-year-old boy Falcon was inside the balloon! He'd been playing in it when it broke free of its tethers and shot off skyward!

Live TV reports followed the balloon as it sailed fifty miles away, in danger of crashing at any moment and turning the kid into something resembling a **chewed up jam sandwich**.

Eventually, the balloon landed with a bump . . . but the boy was not inside! Had he fallen out and ended up **splattered on the ground** like a bug on a windscreen? Nah. Falcon was never in it. He was hiding in the garage at home. **Phew!**

In the aftermath, the family seemed weirdly keen to be interviewed about the incident, and when Falcon was asked why he didn't come out of hiding when they shouted his name he innocently said, 'You guys said we were doing this for the show.' **Say what, kid?**

His parents looked a tad uncomfortable. The next day they appeared on TV again and were asked 'what show?' The dad **squirmed** as he fumbled around inside his own brain for a believable answer. It didn't help matters when Falcon **threw up live on telly!**

It was all a **big fib**, concocted by parents who were desperate to be famous. They'd already had a go on a reality TV show, but wanted more fame, so they thought up the balloon hoax in the hope of getting a bit of media attention – and they got it! Unfortunately for them, they also got in a whole heap of trouble with the law.

What I don't understand about this one is, that kid had a chance to go for an amazing ride around inside a balloon, and didn't take it. Instead, he just hid in the shed or something. If you're going to do a prank, why not do it for real and send the little blighter up into the clouds?

19

Date: 1978
Place: Australia

## SPLATISTICS

| | |
|---|---|
| SILLINESS | (5 splats) |
| IMPACT | (4 splats) |
| DARING | (7 splats) |
| OVERALL | (8 splats) |

# AN AUSSIE ICEBERG? STREWTH!

It sounds like the perfect business idea. Find a huge iceberg in Antarctica, where the water is fresh and pu... Then, tow it to Sydney harbour, chop bits off it and flo... them to the Australians! They'll be queuing round the block, won't they? And the great bit is that no one ow... icebergs so they're free, right? It's a win-win situation

That's what businessman and adventurer Dick Smith decided People laughed and said it was impossible, but Smith pressed o Lo and behold, on 1st April 197... a barge slowly sailed towards th harbour, towing a **giant, white, icy-looking lump** in its wake. O Dick had done it! There he was cruising into port with a massi... iceberg in tow!

Unfortunately, he was just abov to park up outside the Opera House when the skies opened and a downpour of rain began. That's when the prank **fell apa...** It wasn't an iceberg at all. It wa a floating platform covered in a mountain of foam. The rain washed the foam away and, as the tug got closer into view, it grew visibly smaller. **And smaller. And smaller.** Then it was gone. The prank was over. It was a **top effort** though, and no mistake!

**Dennis's Verdict**

It sounds like a ridiculous amount of work went in to creating this prank. I once tried to spray shaving foam over my dad's entire body while he was asleep on the sofa, and that took ages (I got bored and gave up when I reached his middle), so I can only imagine how long this prank must have taken to set up

# OPERATION MINCEMEAT

This is a tale of some very clever thinking. It was the height of World War II, and both sides were hoping for as many lucky breaks as they could get. Then the Germans got one. Drat!

## SPLATISTICS

| | |
|---|---|
| SILLINESS | ☆ |
| IMPACT | ★★★★★★★★ |
| DARING | ★★★★★★★ |
| OVERALL | ★★★★★★ |

a briefcase, said to belong to British officer Major William Martin, were plans to invade eece and Sardinia. Hitler's side got hold of the plans, and moved most of their men in sponse. **The Brits would be walking into a trap!** What a stroke of luck!

least, it would be a stroke of luck if it wasn't for one thing. It was a **brilliant scam**. The lies were actually going to invade Sicily, which was now virtually German-soldier-free. here wasn't a plan to attack Greece or Sardinia at all, and there never was a real Major illiam Martin. The British made up the plan, dumped the fake plans and the Germans l for it **hook, line and sinker**. 'Operation Mincemeat' was a **stroke of genius** and its effect lped steer the rest of the war in our favour.

TOP SECRET

NO PEEKING! PLANS FOR INVASION

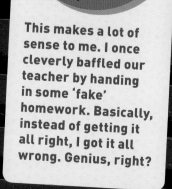

## Minnie's Verdict

This makes a lot of sense to me. I once cleverly baffled our teacher by handing in some 'fake' homework. Basically, instead of getting it all right, I got it all wrong. Genius, right?

# THE WORLD'S GREATEST ARTIST?

Date: 1998
Place: USA

## SPLATISTICS

SILLINESS
IMPACT
DARING
OVERALL

Something you should know about the art world is that, sometimes, it can be a bit on the snobby side. Even Lord Snooty thinks it's a bit much. That might sound like not much fun at all, but look at it this way: wherever anyone needs to be brought down a peg or two, it creates a perfect environment for pranksters.

With this in mind, writer William Boyd and **rock god** David Bowie threw a big party. The idea was to promote a book by Boyd about the eccentric artist Nat Tate. Nat was a **tortured genius** who destroyed his art before completely disappearing in the '60s.

The **arty types** came in their droves, and clapped in appreciation of Nat's work as Bowie read from the book. But get this – **Nat was completely made up!** His name was taken from the British art galleries the National and the Tate.

When Bowie and Boyd came clean, **it put a whole load of snooty noses out of joint.** Rather than admit they'd never heard of Tate, they had pretended they knew all about him, and made themselves look **pretty silly** in the process.

**Minnie's Verdict**

I love it! As I was researching this prank, Mum looked over my shoulder at my laptop screen and said 'Ooh, your Grandad was a successful painter when he was young.' I was amazed! A famous painter in our family! Cool or what? I instantly surfed the net for more information. Disappointingly I just found a small newspaper article about him decorating houses extremely badly.

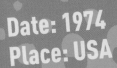

Date: 1974
Place: USA

# VOLCANO HIGH JINKS

MEGA STINK BOMB

## SPLATISTICS

| | |
|---|---|
| SILLINESS | |
| IMPACT | |
| DARING | |
| OVERALL | |

If you lived near a dormant volcano it would always be in the back of your mind, wouldn't it? It could explode at any moment, barfing black smoke into the air and drowning us all in scorching hot lava-goop. Not a good way to go.

That's how it must feel for the people who live next to Mount Edgecumbe in Sitka, Alaska. That one's been dormant for 400 years, but that doesn't mean it can't still **go pop**. And, on 1st April 1974, that was exactly what the locals feared was happening.

Local prankster Oliver 'Porky' Bickar and some chums had used a helicopter to fly **a hundred car tyres** up to the volcano and set them alight, causing a huge amount of black smoke. Porky had been planning the prank for years, but each April Fool's Day had brought lousy, cloudy weather so there wouldn't have been any point. But, on this particular 1st April, the sky was blue and clear – and **the game was on!**

When the Coast Guard flew over the volcano to investigate, they were astounded to see the burning tyres – but not as astounded as they were to see **the words 'April Fool' written in 50-foot letters in the snow!**

It's not often you find a grown-up who (a) thinks of pranks as good as this one and (b) actually has access to a helicopter. So Porky Bickar has to go straight to the top of my Prank Hall of Fame. Even if he does have a silly name.

# THE PILTDOWN LET DOWN

Date: 1912
Place: England

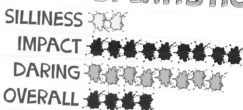

## SPLATISTICS

SILLINESS
IMPACT
DARING
OVERALL

In 1859, Charles Darwin caused a bit of a stir when he wrote a book called *On the Origin of Species*. In it, he claimed humans evolved from apes. These days it's a widely held theory, but back then it blew people's minds.

Ever since then, there's been lots of talk of a so-called '**missing link**' – an animal somewhere between man and ape. And, in 1912, an archaeologist called Charles Dawson claimed he'd found it (or at least some bits of it) in a gravel pit in Piltdown, Sussex. The science world hailed it as the **greatest find in history**. This was proof of our **ape-tastic** roots! For over three decades it seemed like the puzzle was complete. Sorted. Except, it wasn't.

In 1953, scientific research had caught up enough to prove the remains were **fake**. The skull part was an old bit of human bone and the jaw was an orang-utan's, stained to look really old. Dawson was blamed for the hoax, but he died in 1916 so, brilliantly, **escaped a telling off**.

### Dennis's Verdict

Definite bit of monkey business going on there! If there really is a missing link between apes and humans, I wonder if there could also be links between other things. There must be a link between spiders and octopuses! The eight legs thing is a dead giveaway. I think I may also have found a cross between a shrieking howler monkey and a little girl. It's my baby sister, Bea! Now hand over my cash, boffins!

PLUG DOWN MAN?

# DISNEY ON ICE?

## SPLATISTICS

| | |
|---|---|
| SILLINESS | |
| IMPACT | |
| DARING | |
| OVERALL | |

From *Snow White* to *The Lion King*, we all have a favourite Disney story. But the most enthralling one of all could the one about what happened to the Disney founder's body.

Walter Elias Disney, better known as Walt Disney, was born in 1901 in Chicago, USA. He became massively rich and successful when the world fell in love with a **talking mouse** called Mickey and his animation company hit the big time. But, when Walt pegged it in 1966, rumours quickly surfaced that he'd done something a little odd. Apparently, instead of being buried or cremated, **he'd arranged to have his body frozen**.

The story goes that he had himself **bunged in a cryogenic freezer** so that, years later, once the technology had been invented, scientists would be able to bring him back to life. This could have taken a year, or ten, or a thousand – but it wouldn't have mattered, because his body would be perfectly preserved.

Sadly, like so many of our most loved Disney tales, it's a work of **complete fantasy**. Yes, there are some rich stiffs frozen around the world, but not old Walt. He was cremated a few days after he died. It seems there's no **Walt Disney ice lolly** hidden in a cryogenic bunker under the Pirates of The Caribbean ride in Disneyland after all.

**Minnie's Verdict**

Barmy! I'd love to know more about how this would work. I mean, we sometimes have fishcakes in our freezer at home, but when Mum takes them out to defrost them the fish don't spring back to life and start running major film studios. Maybe you're meant to defrost them in the microwave.

25

# FAKING HIS OWN DEATH... BY DYING

Date: 1984 onwards
Place: USA

## SPLATISTICS

SILLINESS
IMPACT
DARING
OVERALL

The American comedian Andy Kaufman found fame in a sitcom called *Taxi* – but it was off-screen where he truly came into his own, bamboozling (and often irritating) his audiences.

He used to **wrestle women** on stage because, by his own admission, he'd stand no chance against men. Then there were the **hoax arguments** he had with people while in the guise of other characters. With Andy, **people never knew what to believe**.

Perhaps the most baffling thing he did was to announce that he was going to **fake his own death**. So, when Kaufman actually DID die of lung cancer in 1984, rumours soon spread that he was still around. Even today, there are those who insist he's still alive – **even including his own brother**.

In 2005 a girl stepped up to say Andy was her father and that he was still living secretly in New York. She was later exposed as an actress who was being paid by someone to keep the rumours alive. **Nice try, though!**

When you think about it, this could be **one of the best pranks ever**. Andy knew he was going to peg it, so he came up with this as a way to carry on baffling people years after he'd gone. Whether you loved or hated him, he was **one of a kind**, as was his final prank.

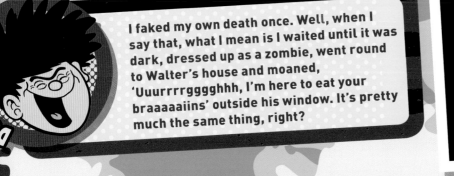

I faked my own death once. Well, when I say that, what I mean is I waited until it was dark, dressed up as a zombie, went round to Walter's house and moaned, 'Uuurrrrgggghhh, I'm here to eat your braaaaaiins' outside his window. It's pretty much the same thing, right?

**Date: 2012**
**Place: England**

# GREGG JEVIN WENT TO HEAVEN

When it was announced on Twitter that Gregg Jevin had died, the World Wide Web was soon buzzing with people offering their condolences. It seemed like everyone knew of Gregg's work and life, and wanted to say how sorry they were he'd died. Sad news. Sad news indeed.

That is, until you realise Gregg **never existed**. Real-life actual comedian Michael Legge made the whole thing up for a giggle. He wrote: 'Sad to say that Gregg Jevin, a man I just made up, has died. #RIPGreggJevin.'

Soon, thousands more had Tweeted that they were sad at Gregg's passing. Legge's fellow comedians joined in the joke, the Radio Times created a spoof schedule for **'Gregg Jevin Night'** and the Royal Albert Hall announced that tickets would soon be going on sale for a **Gregg Jevin memorial concert**. Meanwhile, BBC News sent out the newsflash 'Fictional character Gregg Jevin has died.'

Rest in peace, Gregg. You were a **hero and role model** to all of us.

**Minnie's Verdict**

I'm not a big fan of social networks. What I like is ANTI-social networks. Me and Dennis are trying to set up our own one, so that we can swap minxing and menacing tips. At the moment it's just a long bit of string between our houses, with a plastic cup tied to each end. All the great businesses had to start somewhere though, right?

# FOODIE FAKES

People can be pretty protective of their food – which is probably why it's such a happy hunting ground for pranksters. From spaghetti on trees to cola conflicts, here are some of our all-time favourite food pranks . . .

PEAS

# THE SPAGHETTI HARVEST

Date: 1957
Place: England/Switzerland

## SPLATISTICS

SILLINESS
IMPACT
DARING
OVERALL

Back in the days before the Internet, the BBC was regarded as the finest news service in the world. It was highly respected for its professional standards and impeccable reliabilty . . . so, when the news show *Panorama* broadcast a report on spaghetti growing on trees in Switzerland, it stirred up quite a reaction.

Some viewers rang in to ask if spaghetti could be grown in Britain. They were advised to **plant a stick of spaghetti in a tin of tomato soup** and hope for the best. It was possibly around this point that callers realised they'd fallen for an April Fool's Day prank. There were angry calls too, from people saying the joke shouldn't have been transmitted on a serious show. How could they believe anything the BBC told them ever again? **Harrumph!**

What you have to bear in mind is that, in those days, your average Brit didn't eat **'foreign muck'** like spaghetti or pizzas or lasagne. So, for all many people knew, the story was completely believable. Thankfully, things have moved on since then, and we all know that spaghetti actually comes from bushes, not trees! **Right?**

**Dennis's Verdict**

If spaghetti really did grow on trees, would that mean the meatballs for a spaggy boll would have to be dug up like spuds? I just ask because, if it's anything like Mum's spaggy boll, then you're best off eating the mud instead. The idea of food growing on trees is crazy, isn't it? I mean, I've seen pizza boxes in bushes so maybe it's not THAT crazy, but they're usually empty. Apparently you can also get fruit from trees, but I'm pretty sure that stuff comes from the supermarket.

**Date: 1931**
**Place: USA**

# COLA CLAUS?

Santa Claus. Old Saint Nick. Father Christmas. Kris Kringle. The jolly giftsman goes by many a name, but have you ever wondered why he dresses the way he does? For someone who needs to sneak around late at night on Christmas Eve without being seen, a bright red and white costume seems a bit daft when you think about it.

So why did **Big S.C.** pick that particular get-up? Some believe he didn't. The Coca-Cola Company picked it for him to match their red and white logo. Santa's suit is a marketing tool! **Shocking!** Or at least it would be shocking, if it were true.

Santa Claus is based on a very real figure from the 4th Century, called Saint Nicholas. He was the Bishop of Byra (now Turkey), and by all accounts was a very kind fellow who gave out **loads of prezzies.**

The traditional dress of a Christian bishop of that era was red and white. So, the majority of ancient images of Father Christmas show him in the red suit we know and love today. Perhaps the confusion comes from an ad campaign by Coke that began in 1931 and featured **good old Santa.** It sure worked, as people associate Santa with the **fizzy stuff** to this day – but it doesn't mean they influenced his fashion sense.

I blooming love Santa. He might be an adult, but he's definitely a minx. I mean, while the other adults are always moaning on and on about tidying up, he's running around way past his bedtime and leaving toys all over the place. LEGEND.

*Minnie's Verdict*

SQUELCH ME QUICK!

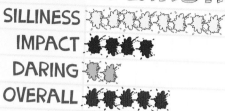

# WHISTLING CARROTS

**Date: 2002**
**Place: England**

## SPLATISTICS

SILLINESS
IMPACT
DARING
OVERALL

We've all heard the old joke . . .

Q. What's the best way to catch a rabbit?
A. Hide in the bushes and make a noise like a carrot.

Arf! But what if carrots really DID make a noise? What if they could whistle to let you know when they're ready for munching? That way, they'd never turn overcooked and mushy ever again! How good would that be, carrot fans? Hmm?

Well, the world's **endless battle** against the carrot cooking problem looked like it could be at an end in 2002. Supermarket Tesco announced they were to start selling genetically-modified carrots that **whistled** when they were done. These super-carrots contained a heat-sensitive gene that opened up holes for air to escape from when the correct cooking temperature was reached. Holes that whistled! So, stick a big pan of them on to boil and, **when you hear a din, it's time for din-dins!**

Presumably this was to be just the start of the musical veg phenomenon. How about **potatoes that yodel? Or peas that sing opera?** And we all know what noise **sprouts** would make the **cheeky pumpy scamps.**

Sadly, it was all just a big prank by Tesco. There's no such thing as whistling carrots, or any other musical veg for that matter. What a tragic end to a **beautiful beautiful dream.**

*Dennis's Verdict*

I reckon all food should tell you when it's done. Bacon that goes 'oink' when it's fried to perfection. Fish fingers that tap you on the shoulder when they're cooked. Maybe even pizzas that fly out of the oven like frisbees straight onto your plate! Mega cool! Come to think of it, sausages already squeal when they're sizzling in the pan, so maybe this one could be a goer after all. I once terrified Walter by telling him the squealing noise was the sound of the pig's ghost escaping.

SPLATISTICS
SILLINESS
IMPACT
DARING
OVERALL

# CRISPS CRUM'S?

Who doesn't love crisps? We all feel that pang of excitement when a huge multi-bag of crisps is first opened, the hidden delights inside spilling onto the floor. Who will be the first to get the roast octopus flavour? Who'll be wolfing down spicy tarantula? Who'll end up stuck with ready salted? It's just like the National Lottery! Only with some crisps.

**Crisps rule.** That's a given. But who do we have to thank for their invention? Well, most **snack historians** (of which there are none) will tell you crisps were invented by George Crum. Crum was a native American chef who ran his own restaurant in New York.

One day, a **troublesome customer** took a dislike to how thick George's chips were, and demanded that they were taken back to the chef to be cut thinner. Crum obeyed, but still the customer complained. Crum cut them thinner again, but still the customer protested! George lost his temper and, to spite the customer, sliced the chips amazingly thin, covered them in salt and fried them until they were **rock hard**. He sent them over to the customer, thinking he'd **storm out**. Instead, the customer **loved them!** Pretty soon everyone wanted this new tasty treat. Great story, but sadly a hoax.

In fact, there were recipes for crisps in many cookbooks long before Crum supposedly invented them. The Englishman William Kitchiner published *The Cook's Oracle* in 1822, which contained the recipe for crisps – though probably the **boring ready salted** variety.

**Minnie's Verdict**

It's only recently I found out that crisps come from potatoes! I just assumed crisps were foot skin scrapings from giants. Now I know they're from spuds dug up from the ground I've gone right off them. Yuck!

# TECHNO TRICKERY

Isn't the Internet brilliant? It's opened up a whole new world of prank potential. But high-tech japery didn't just start when Sir Charles Internet invented the World Wide Web, you know. Here is a bunch of some of history's greatest techno tricks . . .

EXTRA LARDY CRISPS

GASSY FIZZ

# BIG BEN GOES DIGITAL

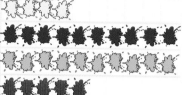

**SPLATISTICS**

SILLINESS
IMPACT
DARING

As far as backfiring jokes go, this one had 'epic fail' written all over it. In 1980, the BBC announced that Big Ben, the world famous clock tower in London, was to have its four faces replaced with digital screens.

The Beeb had expected people to **giggle** at the silly gag, but instead there was an **angry backlash**. How dare anyone even think of messing with such an iconic English masterpiece! The **uproar** was so severe that the claim had to be quickly withdrawn, and the BBC admitted that it was just a joke.

Speaking of iconic bells, a similar prank occurred in America with the **Liberty Bell**, a symbol of freedom and democracy. In 1996 a fast food company called Taco Bell joked that they'd bought the iconic bell and were renaming it the Taco Liberty Bell. The American people were **none too pleased**, and rightly so!

The British Big Ben's original real name was 'The Clock Tower', but it was renamed in honour of Queen Elizabeth's diamond anniversary in 2012. And no, **the Elizabeth Tower will never go digital**. We think.

**Dennis's Verdict**

Daft one, this. What next, turning Buckingham Palace into a coffee chain? Adding a roof on to Stonehenge? Replacing the Queen with a robot? Actually, that last one's not bad.

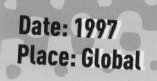
Date: 1997
Place: Global

# INTERNET SPRING CLEAN

A zillion people go online every day, whether it's for sending emails, streaming videos, sharing files, browsing the web or sharing a photo of a kitten peeking out of a swing bin. Aww, just look at the little fella.

In 1997, the net was still young, and people weren't as clever as we are in these days of **online shopping and bin-kittens**. So, when an email went around saying that the Internet was going to **close for twenty-four hours for repairs**, a lot of people were caught out.

The April Fool's jape was actually a revamp of a very old joke about cleaning up the telephone system. For a number of years a gag went round saying the phone network had to be spring cleaned due to **old calls, wrong numbers and engaged tones clogging up the system**. Some gullible folk even believed advice telling them to **place plastic bags over the ear pieces** of their phones to catch the dust that would spray out when the cleaning began. **Brilliant.**

**Minnie's Verdict**

Great example of how pranking moves with the times, this one. In the good old days when the Internet was in black and white, there used to be loads of email pranks flying around. Back then, if you wanted to look at a picture of a kitten peeking out of a bin, it would take nine weeks for it to appear on your screen, and once it did you had to stand up and sing the National Anthem.

**Date: 1962**
**Place: Sweden**

# TIGHTS TV

## SPLATISTICS

SILLINESS
IMPACT
DARING
OVERALL

You have to use your imagination for this one. Imagine you have a telly – but it isn't the wafer-thin, HD, fifty-inch, wi-fi-enabled, cheese-toastie-maker thingy we all have nowadays. It can't even show your fave shows in colour! It's a chunky block with a tiny black-and-white screen that takes forever to even switch on. Well, that's what TV was like when our grannies and grandads were young.

In 1960s Sweden, there was just one TV channel. That's right: one. So, when technical expert Kjell Stennson popped up on that one channel to tell people they could have **free colour telly** by putting a **pair of tights** over the screen, it must have seemed like the future had arrived. He came out with a load of **techno babble** about how the mesh of the tights affected light, prisms and colour spectrums, making the black and white images appear to be in colour.

People all over Sweden rushed about **tearing up stockings and tights** and taping them to their TV screens. They were also told to sit with their heads at **funny angles** for the effect to work better – so they did!

Of course, **it was all a big prank**. Colour telly wasn't in wide use back then and it wouldn't get to Sweden until 1970. The Swedes took it all with good humour though, and to this day it's a fondly told story in the country.

**Dennis's Verdict**

What a brill prank! By the way, have you heard about Smelly-Vision? If you want to sniff the programmes on telly, tie a string around your remote and shove the other end up one nostril. Hey presto! You'll now smell what you see! Best not to put sumo wrestling on, though.

# 18TH CENTURY CHESS ROBOT

## SPLATISTICS

SILLINESS
IMPACT
DARING
OVERALL

In our hi-tech, fancy-pants, 21st Century we can happily play online games and either challenge a friend or play against the computer. But, back in 1770, when Johann Ritter announced that he'd built a chess-playing robot, the world cried, 'You having a laugh, pal?'

'The Turk', as it was called, looked amazing. It was a large wooden box covered in cogs, with the **top half of a mechanical man looming over it.** And a very serious looking fella he was too.

Johann said The Turk could **beat anyone at chess.** It moved of its own accord and those it defeated included Napoleon Bonaparte and the very clever American Benjamin Franklin.

So, how did Johann manage to build a thinking machine that, to this day, hasn't been matched? Well, The Turk was actually **hollow enough to hide a man inside** – and the man chosen for the job was a **brilliant chess player** paid by Johann to win the games. People shelled out to see it as it toured all over the world until, eighty-four years later, it was **destroyed** in a museum fire. Thankfully, no one was in it at the time. Honestly. They **checked**, mate. Arf.

This inspired me to make The Minx, a robotic version of me! Imagine that! I could create chaos in two places at once! I could send The Minx all over the world to spread the minxing word to the four corners of the globe! I rushed to Dad's shed and set about building my automatic mischief android! After ten minutes I got bored and went and got some chips.

**Date: 2000**
**Place: England**

# JELLY BELLY FAT FEET

## SPLATISTICS

| | |
|---|---|
| SILLINESS | |
| IMPACT | |
| DARING | |
| OVERALL | |

People will try anything to lose weight. That said, a lot of Brits manage to lose around forty pounds every four weeks quite easily. All they have to do is join a gym for £40 a month and never go.

So imagine the **wave of excitement** when the *Daily Mail* announced that the Americans had come up with an incredible new invention . . . **'FatSox'**! Socks that literally suck the fat out of your body! Just pop the socks on your feet and **let the magic do its work** as you do some gentle exercise.

Using lots of impressive sciencey words like 'polymers', 'compounds' and 'fat', the article claimed the socks **sucked blubber out of your bloodstream**. Once the socks were full of **lovely wobbly flab**, you simply chucked them in the bin. **Yuck!** But **better out than in**, as Dennis says after eating Windy Beans.

FatSox sounded too good to be true. That's because they were. It was a prank. The compound they talked about, 'Tetrafloramezathine', might have sounded real, but it wasn't. Cue a **world of double chins** juddering with disappointment.

**Dennis's Verdict**

Isn't it a shame there's no such material that can suck fat out of your body? If there was, there would be 'Fat Glovez' for the sausage fingered, 'Fat Trooz' for the tree-trunk legged, 'Fat Hats' for fat heads and 'Fat Pantz' for fat . . . well, you get the idea.

40

# BOOBY TRAP

1980s underwear panic! Aargh! In 1982, the *Daily Mirror* printed a story claiming that a ladies' underwear company had mistakenly put out 10,000 defective bras. They'd accidentally been made with copper wire frames that, while safe for the wearer, were affecting radio and TV signals. The copper was reacting with the women's body heat, creating a static electric charge. Telly and radio programmes were cutting out, and bras were to blame!

It's quite worrying if you think about it. Just imagine watching your fave comedy show, when suddenly a woman wearing a **defective bra** walks past your house. **Zap!** Next thing you know, your TV's changed channel on its own and you're watching a documentary about **Austrian fart otters** migrating to Botswana or something. Thankfully, it was a hoax – and one that loads of people fell for. One **panicking engineer** at British Telecom even demanded to know what make of bra the female staff were wearing!

The following day, the paper admitted that the bra scare was **pants**. It was a prank, and they were sorry. The nation breathed a sigh of relief, knowing its bras were safe. **Phew.**

I shouldn't really say this . . . but I found a bra in a wheelie bin one winter and it made the best double-barrel snowball catapult ever! Not only that, but it made a great set of ear muffs for my journey home.

Minnie's Verdict

# FABLES AND FANTASIES

We'd all love it if ghosts, goblins and fairies were real, right? But if you fall into the trap of actually believing in them, then beware – you're leaving yourself wide open to a pranking!

SLURP! BURP!

TYPE O

# FAIRY NUFF!

## SPLATISTICS

| | |
|---|---|
| SILLINESS | |
| IMPACT | |
| DARING | |
| OVERALL | |

In 1917, two Victorian menaces got people going with a wicked wind-up about finding fairies at the bottom of their garden. Seriously! The cousins, sixteen-year-old Elsie and nine-year-old Frances, produced some photos of themselves posing with proper, actual, real-life fairies! Or, at least, that was what they claimed.

Everyone went **bonkers** and the newspapers of the time raced down to Cottingley, near Bradford, to grab a piece of the elfin action. Stacks of people genuinely believed the girls had fairy friends! Even Sir Arthur Conan Doyle was sucked in, and came out saying he believed the pictures were genuine. And, as Sir Arthur was the big-brained creator of Sherlock Holmes, loads more people joined the fairy bandwagon. **How could it not be true?**

The thing is, the Cottingley Fairies were **utter fakes**. The girls had just cut them out of a picture book, stood them up and posed with the daft things! Best of all, they didn't admit to the jape for **donkey's years**. They were **wrinkly old ladies** by the time they came clean! It was over sixty years later when they finally coughed up the truth. **How's that for keeping a straight face?**

**Dennis's Verdict**

Love it! Cutting out the pictures and standing them up in the ground to look real sort of makes them the original photoshoppers. Elsie and Frances were digital pioneers!

44

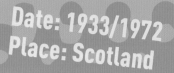

**Date: 1933/1972**
**Place: Scotland**

# BEWARE, THE LOCH NESS HOAXSTER!

## SPLATISTICS

| | |
|---|---|
| SILLINESS | |
| IMPACT | |
| DARING | |
| OVERALL | |

The most famous photo of the Loch Ness Monster is the one called 'The Surgeon's Photo'. You probably know the one. It looks a bit like an elephant scuba diving.

It was taken by a surgeon named Colonel Robert Wilson in 1933. For sixty years it was considered the **strongest evidence of Nessie's existence**. But, in 1994, a chap called Christian Spurling announced that the photo showed nothing more than a **fake monster head attached to a toy submarine**. He was in on the whole thing, along with Spurling's stepdad Marmaduke Wetherell.

That's far from the only Nessie hoax. In 1972, some Yorkshire zoologists claimed they'd found the monster – dead – floating on top of the loch. This time, Nessie turned out to be a dead elephant seal. One of the zoologists, John Shields, had altered it a bit, shaved off its whiskers, then drove up to the loch to dump it. He knew his colleagues were going up there to search for the monster and wanted to play a prank on them. **And a wonderful prank it was, too!**

**Minnie's Verdict**

I thought I'd spotted the Loch Ness Monster once! I leapt into the water and wrestled the beast, clinging to its giant ears while calling for someone to get the press! It turned out not to be Nessie, though. It was Plug from The Bash Street Kids on a swimming lesson. The fact we were at Beanotown Swimming Pool at the time should have been a bit of a giveaway, I suppose.

Date: 1975
Place: USA

# THE AMITYVILLE HORROR

## SPLATISTICS

SILLINESS
IMPACT
DARING
OVERALL

In the 1970s, the Lutz family moved into a house in Amityville, New York. It wasn't long before things got weird. Objects disappeared and reappeared, spooky noises were heard, and everyone had an eerie feeling of being watched. Woooooo!

**Things soon got even odder.** Doors were ripped off hinges. **Goo** dripped from the ceiling. **Scary eyes** were seen peeking in through the window. The family was terrified! Or were they?

Nah. None of it was true. The Lutzes wanted some extra cash so, knowing that the house had a bit of a **grisly past** before they moved in, they decided to make the most of it. A book called *The Amityville Horror: A True Story* was published, and pretty soon Hollywood was making movies about it.

The family even had the place **checked out by 'real' ghost-hunters**, who confirmed it was haunted (so just imagine how daft they must have felt when lawyer and family friend William Weber 'fessed up a few years later).

Researchers have since examined the 'facts' in the aforementioned book, along with the original claims by the Lutzes, and found that pretty much none of it adds up. Still, the only people to suffer are the ones who have bought the house since. To this day, they're still plagued by folk knocking on the door and asking to **meet the ghosts**.

### Dennis's Verdict

Making up ghost stories is a great way to earn extra cash. Once I made up a ghost story about our school being haunted by an evil, two-headed teacher, and then charged people to take them on ghost tours. I got rumbled in the end, when people realised that Mrs Creecher only has one head. And she isn't a ghost. She's not even that scary. Except when she threatens us with extra homework!

DANGER!

# THE CARDIFF GIANT

## SPLATISTICS

SILLINESS
IMPACT
DARING
OVERALL

This prank started in Cardiff (not the one in Wales, but a small area in New York state). When William Newell hired some men to dig a well on his land, they were shocked to discover a body. They were even more shocked when they found that the body was an ancient, ten-foot-tall giant!

Word soon got round, and people were **amazed and fascinated**. They paid Newell fifty cents just to have a quick look at the big horrible thing. **He was raking it in!**

Freak show owner P.T. Barnum offered to buy it for 50,000 dollars, but Newell refused. **Not to be outdone**, Barnum had his own version carved out of stone and claimed that **his** was the real Cardiff giant while Newell's was a fake.

Newell tried to sue Barnum for being a **big fibber** – which was rich coming from him, as he later confessed that his Cardiff Giant was also a fake. His cousin, a tobacconist named George Hull, had had it carved out of a mineral called gypsum, then had it treated with chemicals to make it look ancient. Why? He wanted to **annoy a Reverend** he'd had a barney with a year earlier, and apparently this was the best way to do it!

To this day, Newell's Cardiff Giant remains on display in a New York farmer's museum. No one believes it's real, but it is a **valuable part of pranking history!**

**Minnie's Verdict**

Nice idea! Next time we go to the beach and bury Dad in the sand I'm going to say he's the oldest fossil in the world and the Beanotown museum can buy him for a few quid. Easy money!

# PAUL THE BEATLE IS AS DEAD AS A DODO

BELCH! BAARP!

Date: 1969
Place: USA

## SPLATISTICS

SILLINESS
IMPACT
DARING
OVERALL

The Beatles are the biggest band in the history of pop music. So, when a rumour emerged in 1969 that guitarist and singer Paul McCartney was dead, it soon caught on. The story was that Paul had angrily stormed out of a recording session in 1966, jumped into his car and accidentally crashed and died.

Then comes the mad bit! As The Beatles were raking in so much cash, it was claimed the record company hushed up Paul's demise and hired a **look-a-likey** named William to replace him.

Truth is, **the crash never happened**. This was actually a hoax cooked up by American college students, who cleverly linked lots of bizarre clues to make the whole thing seem plausible. The joke snowballed and soon everyone was looking for clues. For example, people claimed to hear John Lennon saying **'I buried Paul'** in the song 'Strawberry Fields Forever'. What Lennon actually says is **'cranberry sauce'**.

Then there was the famous cover of the *Abbey Road* album, where the band are pictured crossing the street. Some claimed this was a funeral procession with McCartney as the stiff (stood up and walking of course, which is **quite impressive for a corpse**).

## Dennis's Verdict

Don't know about you, readers, but if I was going to cover something up, I wouldn't then go out of my way to leave loads of clues so that people could find out the truth. I reckon some folk have got a lot to learn about the skilful art of pranking!

GOO-! GOO-! SQUELCH!

# FAIRY, FAIRY FUNNY

When you're little, you truly believe there could be fairies living at the bottom of the garden . . . if you're a bit of a softie, that is. But imagine if you toddled outside to look for them and really found one? Well, actually the dead body of one. But it would still be an amazing moment, wouldn't it?

Well, in 2007, a **fossilised fairy** was actually found, or so a popular website claimed. Apparently, the **snuffed-it sprite** was spotted by a dog walking its man on an old Roman road in Derbyshire. When the site made it public, it was inundated with emails asking for more info. Hundreds even wanted to buy it!

For the more reasonable types who saw the pic, there would probably have been three pretty loud alarm bells ringing. Firstly, **fairies don't exist**. Secondly, the website was run by a **prop-maker** called Dan Baines. Thirdly, it was **April Fool's Day!**

Even when Baines eventually came clean and announced that the fairy was a fake, people wanted to get their hands on it. They reckoned he was just back-tracking to **cover up the truth!**

Minnie's Verdict

I would blooming love to discover a magical bunch of fairies living at the bottom of my garden. Don't worry, I'm not going soft. They could be my team of mini-Minnie minxes! Fairies, fetch me my catapult! Fairies, do my homework! Fairies, get me a kebab! BWAH-HA-HA!

# BIGFOOT, BIG FIBS?

## SPLATISTICS

SILLINESS
IMPACT
DARING
OVERALL

Said to live in the colossal forests of North America, Bigfoot (or Sasquatch to his pals) is believed to be a mysterious, ape-like beast who walks on two legs and has magical powers.

In 1967, two cowboys filmed what they claimed was **Biggy** stomping through Bluff Creek on the banks of the Klamath River in California. Roger Patterson and Bob Gimlin claimed they were out riding horses when they stumbled across the creature **squatting near a fallen tree**. Fumbling for his camera (as cowboys do), Patterson began filming it. **The beast gave them a filthy look, before storming off in a huff.**

Lots of folk were **convinced** by the footage, but they were in for a disappointment. In 2008, an old chap named Bob Heironimus came forward and admitted he was the one in the suit. According to Heironimus, the cowboys had offered him cash to put on the suit and **monkey about** while they filmed him. Oh well. **The search continues.**

### Dennis's Verdict

If Bigfoot's so reclusive, how come everyone knows about him? There's even one living in Beanotown Woods. He spends his time juggling tree stumps and doing card tricks. Blooming Bigfoot! Big Show Off, more like. What an abominable showman.

# GHOST TAKES OVER TV!

## SPLATISTICS

| | |
|---|---|
| SILLINESS | 🌸🌸 |
| IMPACT | 💥💥💥💥💥💥💥💥💥💥 |
| DARING | 💥💥💥💥💥💥💥 |
| OVERALL | 💥💥💥💥💥💥💥💥💥 |

*Ghostwatch* could well be the most spectacular (and spooktacular!) TV hoax ever pulled off. It featured ex-*Blue Peter* presenter Sarah Greene reporting live from a family's supposedly haunted home, while chat show legend Michael Parkinson stayed in the studio to talk to experts and take calls from viewers.

At first, the show was light-hearted – but, as the night went on, it became darker, captivating viewing. One of the daughters was attacked by something invisible and left with scratches all over her face. Then, visions of the ghost (named '**Pipes**' by the family) began **popping up** at blink-and-you'll-miss-'em speeds.

**The house was flung into chaos**. Brilliantly, Pipes snuck through the TV signals into the studio and possessed poor old Parky! **Terrifying stuff!** Shame none of it was real.

The whole thing was actually a carefully scripted drama, presented to look like it was all really happening live on TV. There was a **huge outcry** when people found out it was a fake, but only the sourest of sourpusses would deny how **brilliant a prank** it was.

### Minnie's Verdict

I think Pipes might be in my house now. I keep hearing horrifying moans coming from the bathroom. Weirdly, it usually happens on nights when it's been Dad's turn to do the cooking.

# BEASTLY BLUFFS

BASH!

SCARPER

ROADRUNNER

DANGER!

When it comes to animal pranks, all bets are off. Seriously – who'd have thought a hippopotamus was a real thing? That's probably why people actually fell for this collection of wind-ups . . .

# INCREDIBLE FLYING PENGUINS

**Date: 2008**
**Place: Antarctica(ish)**

## SPLATISTICS

SILLINESS
IMPACT
DARING
OVERALL

Those tricksters at the BBC were at it again in 2008. They released a trailer for a new wildlife documentary about the amazing flying penguins of King George Island in Antarctica. These guys didn't bother with all that huddling-to-keep-warm business. Nope, they took to the air and flew to South America to bask in the sun all winter.

It's a shame it was another April Fool's day hoax, as **flying penguins** would be an awesome sight! Then again, you probably wouldn't want them flying over your town, would you? **Imagine the poops from that lot!** Look out below!

For those who remembered the TV comedy show *Monty Python's Flying Circus*, alarm bells would have been ringing as soon as they saw the name of Terry Jones attached to the film. With **comedy legend** Terry involved, **there was bound to be something fishy going on.**

Terry was filmed in fake snow in a London studio, and the flying penguins were expertly animated into the footage. All in all it was **one of the finest hoaxes ever.** As far as uses for penguins go, it definitely beats making them into **chocolate bars,** right?

**Dennis's Verdict**

Us menaces are a lot like penguins, but we don't bother with all that shuffling around in the snow nonsense. If you want to keep warm when it snows, here's my tip: spend your time making LOADS of snowballs, then build a snowball launching machine in time for the next big Beanotown Snowball Battle!

**Date: 1842**
**Place: USA**

# FIJI FISH FINGY

*SMELLY KNICKERS!*

*RAAAZZ!*

## SPLATISTICS

| SILLINESS | |
| --- | --- |
| IMPACT | |
| DARING | |
| OVERALL | |

We all love fish fingers, but this is just mental! American hoax master P.T. Barnum bought what he claimed was a mermaid, and put it in his own museum for public amazement – and disgust.

Barnum put out leaflets showing a drawing of a traditional mermaid, complete with **lady-top** and **fishy-bottom**. Instead, people were treated to an abomination. The 'mermaid' looked like a **horrible cross between Jaws and a chimp**.

Barnum claimed he rented the monstrosity from a Dr J. Griffin of The British Lyceum of Natural History. But, as you've probably guessed, Griffin was also a fraud. He wasn't a Doctor. There never was a British Lyceum of Natural History! His real name was Levi Lyman and he was Barnum's accomplice.

So, just what was the legendary Fiji Mermaid? Well, it was nothing more than the **top half of a stuffed monkey** and the **bottom half of a fish**.

No one's sure where the horrid thing is now. Let's just hope the **rotten fishcake didn't swim away down someone's lav** and is still out there somewhere!

*Minnie's Verdict*

The tricky bit must have been putting the fake mermaid together in the first place. I should know – I tried to make one myself. I used the top half of a teddy bear and taped it to a fish from the chip shop. It fell apart so I stuck the bottom half of the teddy bear on instead. To be honest, it just looked like a worn out teddy bear.

**Date: 1998**
**Place: USA**

# AN OCTOPUS TO LOOK UP TO!

## SPLATISTICS

| | |
|---|---|
| SILLINESS | ✿✿✿✿✿✿✿✿✿✿ |
| IMPACT | ✿✿✿✿ |
| DARING | ✿✿✿✿✿ |
| OVERALL | ✿✿✿✿✿✿✿✿ |

There's nothing more peaceful than a gentle ramble in the woods, is there? Picnics, nature trails, leaf-collecting . . . it couldn't be more relaxing. Until a dirty great octopus leaps at you from high up in the foliage, that is! You'd wet your pants, wouldn't you?

Well, apparently **tree octopuses** can be found in America's Olympic National Forest. Fancily named *octopus paxarbolis*, they like to hang about in tall trees, where they can avoid **Bigfoots** (or should that be Bigfeet?).

Sadly, the Pacific Northwest Tree Octopus isn't real. It was invented by a prankster called Lyle Zapato, who concocted the idea to have **a bit of a giggle**.

It's impossible for an octopus to live outside water, and even if it could it'd be **useless**. The octopus is an invertebrate (which means it has no backbone), so it has to **flop around a lot**. This tends to make tree-climbing difficult, even when you have **marvellous tentacles**. Those tentacles are great at picking stuff up underwater but, without the floaty weightlessness of the deep, they're **as dangly and useless as wet noodles**.

Still, even with the octopus threat averted, you should **always remember to look up when strolling through the woods**. You never know when a bird might be doing its **loo business**, or a squirrel chucking its nuts around. **Ouch!**

**Minnie's Verdict**

Want to make your own tree octopus? Great! Simply attach the pipes from eight vacuum cleaners to a school chum, and then cover the rest of that chum in whelks. Then ask him to stand next to a tree and wait to be discovered by science boffins. Look out for Bigfoot though!

**Date: 1931**
**Place: Isle of Man**

# GEF THE TALKING MONGOOSE

WINDY BEANS

## SPLATISTICS

| | |
|---|---|
| SILLINESS | ★★★★★★★ |
| IMPACT | ★★★★★ |
| DARING | ★★★★★ |
| OVERALL | ★★★★★ |

When Mr and Mrs Irving and their thirteen year old daughter Voirrey told folk of their new friend Gef and how clever he was, it probably didn't sound all that unusual. However, when the Irvings mentioned that Gef was a talking mongoose who lived in the walls of their farm house, it became a bit more odd.

Gef said he was an **'extra extra clever mongoose'**. He thought it best that they never lay eyes on him, as the sight might cause them to go **insane**. So, with no thought for his own wellbeing, Gef remained inside the walls.

The press got hold of the story and **soon the world was talking about Gef the talking mongoose**. People came from all around to meet Gef, but he always proved elusive and shy. Paranormal investigators came and went, with little or no proof of Gef's existence.

After a few years, the Irvings moved out of the farm. The next owner claimed he'd shot and killed Gef and wanted to show off the body for cash, but the creature he produced looked nothing like the family's description. **Phew!**

Right up to her death in 2005, Voirrey still claimed Gef was real. But was he? **Let's hope so!**

Wow Pa, a talking animal!

Hello!

**Dennis' Verdict**

My dad once met a talking horse. His car broke down and this brown horse walked out of a field and told him what was wrong with it. Dad was terrified, but followed the brown horse's advice and drove off to the nearest police station. The copper there said he was lucky he hadn't met the grey horse! Dad asked why, and the policeman said, 'The grey horse doesn't know anything about cars!'

# THE DOGS ARE ALL WHITE

Date: 1965
Place: Denmark

## SPLATISTICS

SILLINESS
IMPACT
DARING
OVERALL

This story, published in Danish newspaper *Politiken* in 1965, must have left dog owners feeling seriously ruff! (Get it? 'Ruff'? Like the noise dogs make? Oh, forget it.)

The paper claimed that the Danish government was **demanding all dogs be painted white.** The thinking was, dogs keep getting involved in traffic accidents (and **none of them know the Highway Code**), so something had to be done to make them more visible. And what's the best way of doing that? **Give 'em a lick of paint, that's what!**

Of course, it's not true. Coating every dog in paint would be both cruel and impossible. It turned out to be nothing more than an **April Fool's giggle** – but just imagine if the idea had caught on! Household paints would have been renamed things like 'Alsatian White' or 'Pooch Pastel Cream'.

Come to think of it, if you're going to paint your **bow-wow** white, you may as well let the **soggy doggy** run riot around your house and give your walls a freshen up in the process. **Wall-kies!**

## Dennis's Verdict

This reminds me of the time Gnasher wrecked the shed and tipped a full tin of white paint over himself. At first he was a bit miffed about it, but when he realised people were running away because they thought he was some sort of hairy dog-ghost, he loved it. He haunted everyone in Beanotown every night for a week. That's my boy!

PAINT

FLOUR

Date: 1874
Place: USA

# ZOO MUST BE JOKING!

A New Yorker ran down the street, clutching a newspaper and looking utterly terrified. 'All the animals have escaped from the zoo!' he cried. 'Run! Run for your lives!'
'Which way?' yelled another.
'The same as me! I'm not chasing the rotten things!'

OK, so that probably didn't actually happen, but there really was **panic on the streets of New York** when the *Herald* newspaper announced that **every beast in the Central Park Zoo had got out.**

According to the story, fifty people had been **gobbled up by various critters.** Mothers rushed to get their children out of school. Men barricaded their houses. Some people took to the street armed with guns, looking to shoot the first **bear, wolf or sealion** they came across.

Oddly it wasn't an April Fool's gag this time (it was the middle of November!). So, at the time, a lot of people fell for it. Those who read the article all the way to the bottom, though, were relieved to see one thing: **a confession that the entire story was a massive hoax.**

Minnie's Verdict

I love the idea of zoo animals tearing around all over the place. Just imagine it: lions running through the school playground, badgers splashing around the local swimming pool, massive fish flopping about the High Street doing their shopping. Minx heaven!

SQUELCH!

59

# FINDING THE FAKES

Woah there, little horsey! You've not finished your Prankipedia yet! Oh no siree Bobkins. Before you go, there are a few things you should know to stop yourself from being pranked. You see, there are a few so-called 'facts' out there that people will try to make you believe, but they're actually nonsense! Twaddle! Flibble-flabble! Beanotown-babble!

Fortunately, Roger the Dodger and Plug have put their mind-boxes together to come up with this handy list of debunks and fake-busters. Read up on them now, learn them with your head, and become a right little prankspert!

## A tooth in a fizzy drink will dissolve overnight

**Possible Story:** This kid drank fifty fizzy drinks before bed. When he woke up his skeleton had dissolved. They push him around in a wheelbarrow now.

**THE TRUTH!** Not so much tooth rot as tommy rot! Fizzy drinks will NOT dissolve teeth. There's a lot of sugar and yucky chemicals in them, but not THAT much!

**Dodger's Debunks**

**Plug's Fake Facts**

### Eating carrots makes you see in the dark

Nope. They do contain vitamin A which is good for eyes, but not enough for infrared vision. Mind you, ever seen a rabbit with a torch? Hmm?

**Dodger's Debunks**

## Peeing in swimming pools turns the water blue

**Possible Story:** This boy widdled in a pool and the water went blue. Everyone in the water got stained and, ten years later, they're still blue! Now they all look exactly like Smurfs.

**THE TRUTH!** Sadly not true. There is no such dye in swimming pools that turns any colour if you wee in it. That said, please don't do it. Especially not from the top board.

## We accidentally swallow at least eight spiders in our lifetimes

**Possible Story:** A woman was asleep with her mouth open and a family of spiders ran inside her mouth and set up home. They now legally own the woman. She lives in a big web and pays the takeaway shop thousands to put dead flies on her pizzas.

**THE TRUTH!** It's rubbish. Never happens! In fact, a journalist invented this to specifically prove a theory that people will believe anything.

### All bats are blind

Most bats can see perfectly well. They use their unique hearing like sonar to hunt, as it's more efficient. That's why they make softie squeaks!

### If you wake a sleepwalker up they will die!

Why would they? If someone was walking in their sleep and you shook them awake, they'd simply be confused and wonder where the duvet was.

### If you crack your knuckles you'll get arthritis

There's no evidence to say you'll get arthritis (hardening of the arteries) in your hands if you insist on cracking your knuckles. It is a bit horrible though.

## Chain letters and emails carry real curses

**Possible Story:** My friend's friend got an email saying if she didn't pass it on to thirteen people something bad would happen to her. The second she deleted the email her computer electrocuted her – to death!

**THE TRUTH!** Stupid chain letters have been going round for centuries. Nowadays, they're online. Usually they say you have to give money to someone or you'll suffer a curse. It's nonsense. Ignore it.

## 'Jedi Knight' is a recognised religion

**Possible Story:** An R.E. teacher in a London school is a proper Jedi Knight and he can legally cut naughty kids in two with a lightsaber.

**THE TRUTH!** 'Fraid not. Some people have put 'Jedi' on forms asking what religion they are, but they may as well have put 'nutter'.

## You can see the Great Wall of China from the Moon

Not with the naked eye you can't! No astronaut ever said that, and it's nowhere near big enough to be seen from over 230 thousand miles away. Lunacy!

## Eating cheese before bed gives you nightmares

**Possible Story:** Thirty years ago, a French bloke ate a mountain of cheese before bed and now he's still asleep, trapped in a three-decade-long horror film of his own creation – inside his mind!

**THE TRUTH!** Quite the opposite. Most dairy products contain an acid called tryptophan that has a calming effect. Ring Dennis or Minnie before bed if you want nightmares.

## A sticky siuation!

**Possible Story:** A good friend of ours was the champion of his school's bubblegum bubble-blowing contest (try saying that quickly!). It was the final round, and he was in the middle of blowing the world's most gigantic bubble, when suddenly he sneezed and accidentally swalled the gum! GULP! It went all gooey and stuck to his insides, and didn't come out for seven years!

**THE TRUTH!** It's true that our bodies can't break down bubblegum, but it still makes its way through our systems – and it definitely doesn't take seven years. In fact, you'd probably see it next time you go to the loo!

## Plug's Fake Facts

### Humans only use 10% of their brains

We use most of our brains all the time, but just aren't conscious of it. We move, breath, remember and decide loads of things without realising.

## Dodger's Debunks

### Mixing popping candy and cola will kill you

**Possible Story: A really strict school said the naughty kids could have popping sweets and cola if they signed a contract saying they'd behave. They did so and guzzled it all down. Less than ten minutes later, each of them had exploded into tiny pieces because of the chemical reaction. And it was ALL legal!**

**THE TRUTH!** There isn't enough gas produced from either the sweets or the cola to produce anything more than a burp.

GASSY FIZZ

## Dodger's Debunks

### There are alligators in the New York sewers

**Possible Story:** There's only three tramps left in New York because the 'gators ate the rest!

**THE TRUTH!** No alligators have ever lived in the N.Y. sewers, and no one ever bought a bunch of them as pets and then flushed them down the loo when they got too big. What a croc!